NANTUCKET
THE OTHER SEASON

NANTUCKET
THE OTHER SEASON

Photographs and Text by Stan Grossfeld

Introduction by David Halberstam

The Globe Pequot Press   Chester, Connecticut

Library of Congress Catalogue Number 82-081182
ISBN 0-87106-971-7

Printed in the United States of America

First Edition
Second Printing

Cover and Book Design by David Ford

To mother Mildred and sister Sandy,
who taught me more than any book.

INTRODUCTION

For most people Nantucket is a summer place. It sits off the Cape, a small, almost self consciously quaint island of about 5,500 people, no more than a third of them in the real estate business, and with the approach of summer it suddenly swells to a noisy boisterous small city of 35,000 people. Restaurants and wine stores, closed over the off-season, bloom again; glass whales are dusted off and placed in the windows of souvenir shops. The tourists themselves are eagerly awaited and they do not disappoint; they arrive, every year in greater numbers, only to be scorned by the locals for their trouble.

In the A&P and the Hub, the downtown centers of both commerce and gossip, the local residents and the long time summer residents (who, out of each other's presence, normally complain about each other) curse the tourists and the newcomers; this year, they always say, is worse than last. More, August is worse than July (though the July people are often cursed for not having as good manners as the August people). Everyone longs for the good old days of the past; this includes those who arrived in say, 1972, when people were of course already disenchanted with the present and longing for the good old days. The island is crowded, there are too many cars, and sometimes one has a sense that if it were physically possible, Nantucket might sink under the weight of all of this; instead what is more likely is that it will simply run out of fresh water.

By the second week of August things are frenzied. The thousands of college students who form the migratory labor class in the new summer affluence and who have promised to stay on to Labor Day, begin to quit their jobs. Groups form to do something about the dog problem on the island. Other groups form to do something about the traffic problem. Tempers are short. Somewhere in all this, often ignored in the mass of humanity and the rising sense of the island's social status, are beautiful beaches, lovely moors, sunsets at Madaket worthy of setting back the dinner hour. Though it is vacation time there seems to be less and less time to spend simply enjoying what nature has bestowed and what man is intent on devouring. Miraculously, the summer passes and the tourists are mostly gone and so are most of the summer people. The Island returns to itself, once again a small town with small town rhythms; plumbers come when called; almost the whole community assembles regularly on Saturday mornings for the high school football games. Locals and long time summer residents congratulate themselves on having survived another season: the time between Labor Day and Columbus Day, they assure each other, is the best season of the year. People are once again not only courteous with each other, but even with tourists. The weather is almost lyrical. Then slowly, this too changes. October is the month which betrays. In late October the days go more quickly.

By November the trees become bare and they reveal a different town. Only now with the rich foliage gone, can the true simplicity of the local architecture be seen and appreciated. Darkness comes earlier, and even in early evenings the town is eerie. For the homes even in the center of town are barely lit. Electricity on Nantucket is dear, expensive enough to warm the heart of the coldest Sheik. Once the town was noisy, now it is often curiously still, as if resting from a time in which far too much commerce was transacted in far too small a place over much too brief a time.

Of Nantucket's seasons I love the fall the most, and I know the winter least well. It arrives with a rawness, cutting through even the warmest of clothes. I have only spent a little time in Nantucket during the winter, yet even then I have witnessed the small miracle of watching a pheasant strut across my yard near the center of town and drink from my backyard pond; comparably, I have eaten scallops taken out of the bay that very day, a pleasure almost equally miraculous. But it is a time and place I do not know well. It is Stan Grossfeld's special gift that he has caught and preserved this secret time in an uncharted place. Usually photos of Nantucket are taken by summer soldiers, and they run to a type: dories on a secluded beach, fog rolling in to cap the moors, endless seagulls playing on the pier.

Grossfeld's photos are of a different place, an island closer to its past, still untouched and uncorrupted. They tell their own truth, of a surviving simplicity of life, and for that and for the eloquence of his work I pay him the highest compliment a long time resident can make: his photos took me where I had never been on territory I thought was mine.

— David Halberstam

FOREWORD

Soon after the summer's final ferry is launched and headed for Cape Cod, there's an old story they like to tell in the Pacific Club on Nantucket. A restaurant owner goes down to meet the Steamship on a summer day, spies a particularly large crowd, and yells back to his chef, "Put more water in the chowder."

The story always gets a good laugh from the Islanders at the Pacific for they, better than anyone, know that Nantucket in the summer is, in a sense, watered-down chowder. As tourists and their mainland problems and pressures invade this six-by-sixteen-mile island, thirty miles off the coast of Cape Cod, the pace of the island quickens. The rhythms change.

But it is when the tourists have left, when the resident population slips from 35,000 to 5,500, that the other Nantucket, the real Nantucket, comes out of hiding.

If you want Chinese food during the off-season, you are on the wrong island. The closest sparerib is across Nantucket Sound, and the airport is closed for the night. If you get a Big Mac attack, gargle with salt water.

By the first game of the World Series in October, Main Street will be naked of vehicles at night. By December, fifty-five Christmas trees will line the cobblestone streets. Snowfall in Nantucket most years is sparse — it may snow several inches at night and melt away by noon. But in the deep-freeze period of January some people refer to Nantucket as the Rock, because Old Man Winter can make escape impossible for a time.

Daffodils planted by the hundreds in the fall blossom in April. And just when the Islander begins regretting those nasty things he said about the tourists, they come back like locusts. Once again, the island swells with arriving newcomers and a frenetic pace of life takes over.

This book is an attempt to capture the spirit of life on Nantucket in the off-season.

— Stan Grossfeld
February 14, 1982
Nantucket, Massachusetts

FALL

Nantucket's five selectmen know when it's autumn: complaints about noisy drinking establishments stop piling up on their desks.

They then turn to other matters. And because Nantucket is both a town and a county, the selectmen double as county commissioners. When the selectmen of Nantucket need approval of the county commissioners, they talk to themselves.

Usually they meet in a small hearing room before a handful of people. One week in September, Shellfish Warden Allen Holdgate suggested decreasing the number of scalloping days in a week from six to five, to protect the industry. The selectmen ruled that, henceforth, there would be no scalloping on Mondays in addition to Sundays.

The following week, Selectmen Chairman Kenneth Holdgate, Jr., the warden's nephew, had to move the meeting upstairs to the roomier courtroom after irate scallopers brought in a hundred and fifty signatures protesting against elimination of one weekday to ply their trade.

1

"If we must reduce the number of days we go scalloping to five days per week, we would like to have it the same as other businesses (plumbers, carpenters, masons, electricians, etc.), Monday through Friday," the petition stated.

Some of the full-time scallopers were worried. The previous year, hundreds received calls from the Internal Revenue Service about their reported incomes. This year, at least, they wanted a little representation with their taxation.

Warden Holdgate, seventy-one, a fisherman for forty-two years and shellfish warden for seventeen, is well respected for his fairness. One year he fined his brother-in-law, nephew, and uncle for having dredges overboard before the 6:30 A.M. starting time. Another year he caught a scalloper fishing without a license. The residents of Our Island Home benefited from the two boxes of scallops Holdgate confiscated.

After an hour's debate, the selectmen compromised on the issue. They reinstated the Monday-through-Saturday schedule but cut the bushel limit from six per man, twelve per two-man boat, to five per man and ten per boat. The compromise was not reached without some grumbles about patronizing the Saturday scalloper and, worse still, letting the money go "'round Brant Point" with Off-Islanders.

Two months later the selectmen amended their amended ruling and restored the "six-twelve" limits.

*   *   *

On Straight Wharf in autumn, functional wooden scalloping boats replace sleek white fiberglass hulls of recreational sloops and cabin cruisers.

On Main Street, fresh produce and flowers from one of the island's three farms are still sold in the morning — at least until Thanksgiving.

At Bartlett's Ocean View Farm, the self-service produce stand too is filled with vegetables. Phil Bartlett keeps about ten dollars there for customers to make their own change. Money has never been stolen.

Spiritually, Bartlett says, he feels better when the tourists leave. "They seem to be younger, richer, and pushier every year," he says. "But September's a better month

than July. There's more variety of corn and tomatoes."

Ocean View Farm is two-hundred acres but it's not for sale. "I could get six million dollars for it. But I have three boys and one girl. What are they gonna have? No, I'm not going to sell out to the clique of lawyers and builders. They're all tied together.

"I enjoy it here; it's a better life. The kids aren't exposed to the everyday bad things on the mainland. But it's hard for them, too, because there's nothing to do," Bartlett observes. "The schools are good, though. Did you see Saturday's football game? My kid scored the winning touchdown in overtime!"

*   *   *

Standing in the end zone of the football field, Coach Vito Capizzo runs the Nantucket Whalers through scrimmages, occasionally glancing at his watch. One player is late, for which he pays a price. Capizzo orders him to do "one up, one down" for each minute he is late.

When Capizzo arrived in Nantucket in 1964, after thinking the job offer was for Nantasket, he inherited a hapless team of fifteen players who still wore leather helmets and played only four games.

Three years later, his team was undefeated, and later won 23 games in a row and a 1980 division Super Bowl.

"It's a unique situation here," says Capizzo. "Last year, of a hundred and fourteen boys in the school, ninety went out for football."

When the Whalers returned from their Super Bowl victory on the mainland, the entire team was escorted down Main Street by police and fire trucks, sirens wailing, lights flashing, band playing. They had beaten a tough team from East Boston.

Playing for Nantucket has its special complications. When the Whalers play away, they always pay their respects to Nantucket's moody weather by leaving the day before the game. The team stays in a motel overnight under the watchful eyes of the coaches.

Visiting teams stay in local guest houses or homes. Coach Capizzo remembers one stay that was longer than usual. "Blue Hills (near Boston) came here and played. Then a nor'easter hit and they were stuck. Seventy kids and ten cheerleaders. That's when I got the big pot out, and made the spaghetti sauce."

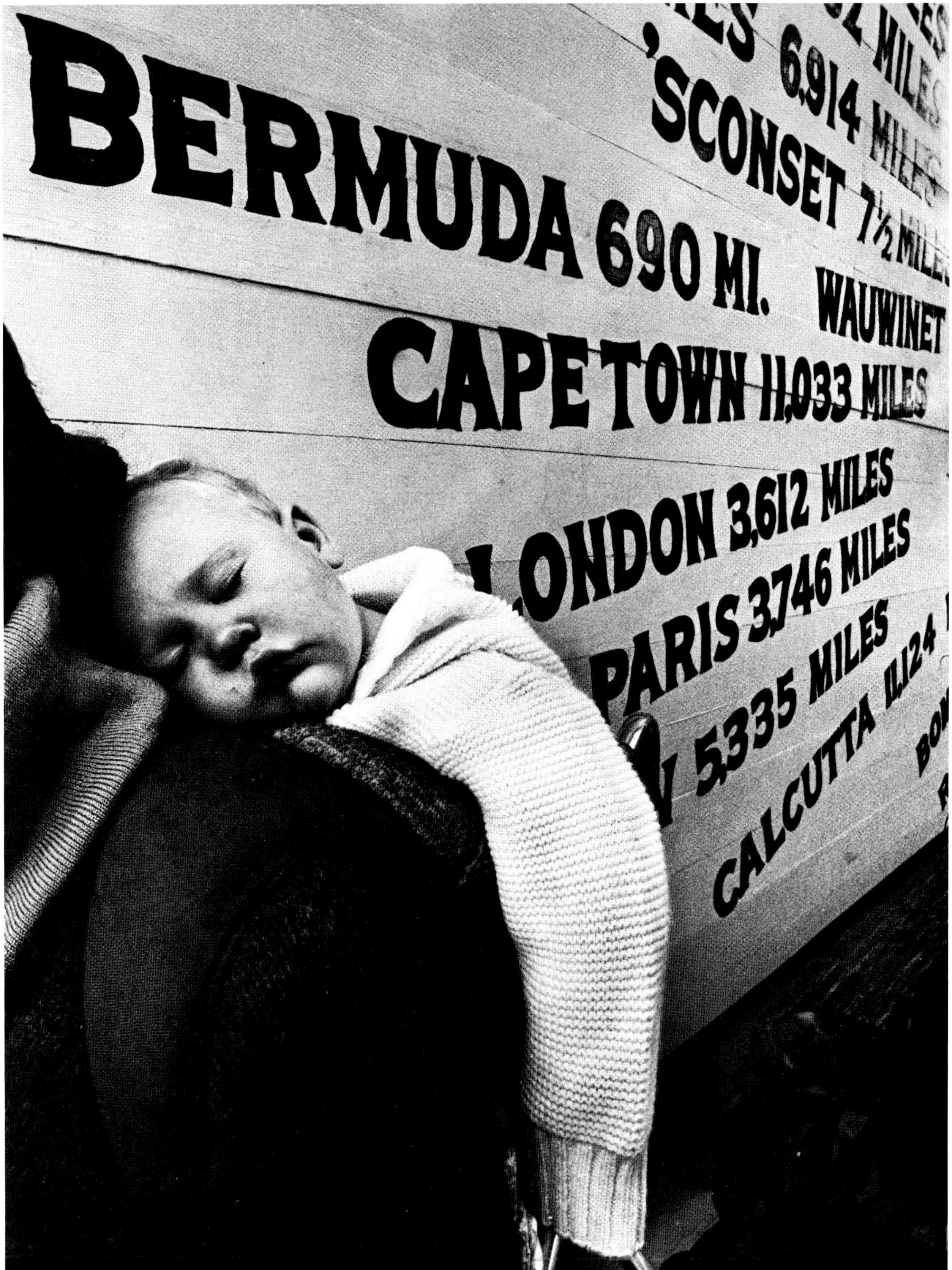

'SCONSET 7½ MILES
BERMUDA 690 MI.
WAUWINET
CAPETOWN 11,033 MILES
LONDON 3,612 MILES
PARIS 3,746 MILES
5,335 MILES
CALCUTTA 11,124

20

SAM

Sam Cockcroft was not the first to seek free lodging amid the Chippendale, Sheraton, and American Federal furniture at the historic Jared Coffin House.

But he was the first to succeed. "The first few times he strode in here, we threw him out," recalled Frances Bain, who handles the hotel's reservations.

"Oh, other cats have tried," Bain continued, "but they always made the fatal mistake of going in the dining room and bothering the guests. Not Sam. That's when I noticed he was special."

Special, indeed. Special enough to persuade Cynthia Cockcroft, his owner, to leave him in Nantucket while she wintered in Virginia and Bermuda; special enough to be a welcome, unpaying seasonal guest, and special enough to be the only surviving member of his litter.

Sam, with apple-green eyes, neatly groomed hair, a heart-shaped face, and luxurious whiskers, is one of a litter of six kittens struck with an intestinal disease, enteritis. When the disease was discovered, Cynthia took them to the best veterinarian she could find.

The veterinarian advised that they all

be put to sleep. Cynthia, near tears, agreed. Twenty minutes later, the veterinarian returned with one ginger-colored kitten in his palm.

"I couldn't do this one," he told her. "He's spunky. He might live."

Sam has lived, and learned to live in luxury.

Several years ago, Sam was such a nervous wreck after traveling to Nantucket from Virginia that Cynthia vowed not to put him through that ordeal again as long as she lived on Nantucket.

"I love Sam. I treat him like a human being. I miss him terribly, but I let him stay here," she said. "He hates to fly so."

At the end of that summer, she gave her next-door neighbor, Carol Briggs, five cases of cat food — and Sam. But cohabitation with the Briggs's female cat didn't please Sam, and he packed up and began casing the town.

When Cynthia called from Bermuda to check on Sam, he was found at the Coffin House, which was built in 1845 by Jared Coffin, one of the island's most successful shipowners. The message relayed back to Bermuda was brief: "Leave Sam alone. He's got the poshest spot on the island."

One day, a fire alarm wailed from downtown. The guests at the Coffin House smelled the thick smoke and scurried down the nine steps that led out of the old brick building.

Seconds later, the stately atmosphere of the Coffin House was transformed into a whirl of galloping firemen, stretching hoses and clanging ladders.

"Chimney fire," Chief Bruce Watts told his men. "Let's check every room that the chimney goes through."

The firefighters had moved rapidly through all the rooms when one spotted the only guest still in the hotel. Sam lazily opened one eye and sized up the group of firefighters. Then he curled up a bit, slipped his head over one tucked-under paw, and went back to sleep.

Sam established himself as "the king of the Coffin House, protecting his domain," Bain said. "One day a black dog came in and jumped on Sam's chair. Sam chased that dog out of the living room, into the hallway, out the door, and all the way down Broad Street toward Main Street. I thought Sam was going to get the worst of it. But all you could hear was that damn dog yelping."

One winter day, a new desk clerk received a package addressed to Sam Cockcroft, c/o Jared Coffin House, Nantucket Island, Massachusetts. The clerk dutifully went to the guest registration book, but found no Sam Cockcroft listed. She checked future reservations, also to no avail. Someone went by and explained to her, "That's Sam the cat, you dummy!" She opened the package in front of Sam. It contained a toy velvet mouse sent by Cynthia from Bermuda.

As with many Nantucket residents, the hordes of summer were not appreciated. "As soon as there's a group around," said manager Phil Read, "Sam gets up and leaves. I leave the manager's door ajar for him."

"The only time Sam will tolerate a crowd is during Christmas Stroll week," added Bain. "He sits by the reception desk and allows himself to be petted by our summer guests who come back for the Christmas holiday."

The time came, however, for Sam to move on. Cynthia sold her Nantucket home and prevailed on a "most indignant" Sam to move to Virginia with her.

"Sam always reminded me of an aristocratic club member sitting in the same chair day after day," said Bain. "Sam's a very classy cat. He'll always be welcome here."

MADAKET MILLIE

"Get the hell outta here," snapped Mildred Jewett shortly before delivering a surprise right jab to my windpipe.

"I am sick and tired of people coming around and telling me that I'm a legend and wanting to take my picture. Well, no pictures and I don't change my mind. Take my picture," she growled, "and I'll have your damn camera."

Mildred Jewett, a/k/a Madaket Millie, or simply Millie, was denying the truth: She *is* a living legend on Nantucket.

Built low to the ground like a fullback, with muscular arms and a stormy orange face, Millie has little patience for prying reporters, photographers, and most two-legged tourists. It took many visits over many months, a loaf of cranberry nut bread on her birthday ("Is this a bribe or a come-on?" she said, tossing it onto a pile of debris inside her house), and glossy prints of Snoopy, her white German shepherd, to get a half-smile, a handshake, and, finally, an invitation into her house.

But her irascible demeanor disguises the warm heart she has for animals, the Coast Guard, helicopters, the wind, the

sea, coffee ice cream, and children.

She doesn't discuss her past, nor does she permit herself to be photographed. She's no dummy, either. She once detected that I was not only tying my shoelaces but also sneaking photos of the three-legged cat napping on her foot.

Millie, who turned seventy when the twentieth century turned eighty, learned early how to take care of herself. Her mother deserted the family when Millie was just six months old. Although a loner, she was quite close to her father until he committed suicide in 1955.

In the early days, Millie used to climb onto the roof of her house on Nantucket's west end, where she would watch the sea. In 1947, the Coast Guard closed down its Madaket station. That very same day, Millie spotted the freighter, *Kotor*, aground in the dense fog off Madaket. The captain thought he was stuck on a shoal forty miles southeast of Nantucket. It was Millie's S.O.S. to the Coast Guard's Brant Point station that sent help.

During World War II, Millie trained dogs for military assignments, for which an appreciative Coast Guard made her an honorary warrant officer of the highest rank.

Long after the Coast Guard abandoned its Madaket post, Millie has faithfully kept watch over the west end of the island. Perhaps to let the world know that protective vigilance would continue there, the Coast Guard gave Millie a sign, West End Command, which is nailed over the front door to her small weatherbeaten house.

Millie's house is protected by an early warning system of dogs and ducks. Until recently, her bed was a mattress on the floor. Her living room, with the venetian blinds pulled tight, has so little light that her indoor plants deserve some kind of horticultural survival award. Her electricity meter is usually at a virtual standstill.

During a recent cleanup of her house, her Coast Guard friends discovered a flea marketful of memorabilia, including a membership card for the Shadow Club, mailed with a 1½ cent postage stamp; a World War II honorable discharge certificate from the U.S. Army for her dog, Buddy; and a sepia-toned 1937 Associated Press photo of a smiling Amelia Earhart sitting in her plane at the start of her ill-fated around-the-world flight.

At Madaket, Millie calls her own shots. One windy fall day, the Brant Point station called to tell her to put up the small craft warnings. She had already done it.

"I decide when it's rough, and I decide when to take them down," she said.

She is as protective of her privacy as she is of the island. During one of my early visits to her, I asked what had happened to her cat with three legs and a mangled paw. "He didn't tell me and I didn't ask," she said. Then she unloaded: "I was having a nice day until you showed up. I don't like you. There is no in between. You either like people or you don't. At least I tell you to your face. Even if you were president of the United States, I would tell you to your face."

Residents, however, see Millie's other side. Pick a day, or night, and she'll have offered advice on how to fix a broken scallop dredge or assisted motorists whose vehicles got stuck in the sand. "Underneath, there's a big heart," says Chief Paul Boucher at the Brant Point station. "She would do anything for anyone who needed it."

Lillian Waine, a newscaster for Nantucket's only television station, recalled Millie's response when Lillian's cocker spaniel puppy, Bonnie, was hit by a car on a Sunday afternoon. When Lillian, five children, and Bonnie went looking for help, the local Society for the Prevention of Cruelty to Animals hospital was not open. But Millie's heart was.

"I was scared stiff of her, the old bat," Lillian recalled. "It was terrible. The kids were screaming. Bonnie was whining. Millie must have had at least thirty dogs then and a pet seal. Her dogs were all barking.

"Millie came out and wanted to know what the hell I wanted. 'Keep those goddamned kids quiet and maybe we'll do something,' was her way of saying hello.

"Then she turned and looked at Bonnie. Her whole being changed. She took off her jacket and placed it on the hood. In absolute silence she worked on the dog. She manipulated Bonnie's hipbone back into its place. You could see the tremendous love in her eyes."

When Lillian asked how much she owed, Millie was direct: "Not a goddamned thing. Keep her out of the road, that's all."

Millie was married once, but all she will say about it is that her husband was from Yonkers and it didn't work out.

But Millie's love for the island, and her role as guardian of the west end, have continued. At the Brant Point station she has her own inscribed coffee cup. And every week, the Coast Guard picks her up and drives her to town for groceries.

At the A&P, wearing a green Coast Guard jacket that says West End Command in large black letters on the back, she is treated like a celebrity. The butcher saves all the best bones for her precious dogs. She hands the market manager a pile of money and coupons. The Coast Guard takes her food through the checkout, then drives her home.

Most of the groceries are for her animals. When she gets home, she stands on the front steps and announces, "Okay you guys, it's food time. Come on, come on up." With that, a half dozen ducks, several Canada geese, and a couple of gulls arrive. Millie, in her daily ritual, feeds them fresh bread, which they nibble from her hand.

Several Nantucket seasons after Millie took her first swipe at me, she softened. She invited me into her house and, as if to congratulate me for persistence, she offered her hand in friendship. "I've had to fight since my mother left when I was six months old," she explained. "And I'm still fighting today. Nothing good comes easy."

SCALLOPS

Tom Larabee tugged the scallop dredge back toward the boat. Tom Jr. poured piping hot coffee from a thermos, the warm steam rising in his cold face. It was raining like hell and the harbor was rough. The younger Larabee, twenty, had been having thoughts about getting off the island and into the real world. (A year later he was a U.S. Marine.)

The pelting rain ran down Tom Sr.'s face, racing between the wrinkles of his forehead and forming droplets on his nose. High winds blew them back to sea. "I love a nor'easter," he said as he flipped the two-hundred pounds of metal, sea-weed, and sweet Nantucket bay scallops onto the culling board. A harvest.

Tom Sr. reached for a scallop that had the growth ring of a mature adult scallop. He removed his orange utility gloves and reached inside the rain parka for his pocket knife.

The other scallop shells were snapping, crackling, and popping open and shut in the background. Tom Sr. opened one and pointed to the various parts. "That's the marshmallow. The good part. It's really the muscle of the scallop."

He pointed to all the yucky stuff around the muscle. "This is the guts," he said. "And see these dots along the edge of the shell. These are the eyes."

Twenty-eight pairs of iridescent eyes stared at the visitor. Like the eyes at Wimbledon courtside, they shifted as the visitor moved nervously from side to side.

To the rookie scalloper, for whom rolling eyes in a scallop shell are trouble-some, the arithmetic is downright horri-fying: Each scallop has about 56 eyeballs and each bushel has about 350 scallops, and so the observant scallop opener makes eye contact roughly 19,600 times per bushel. That's slightly more eyes than there are seats at a New York Knicks game at Madison Square Garden.

With a legal limit for a two-man crew of 12 bushels, we're talking about catching the glint of some 235,200 beady, salty eyes about the size of the black vanilla beans in Breyer's ice cream.

As if to break the stare of all those eyes, the boat swerved left to avoid crossing lines with another scalloper. The scallop eyes were gone now and Tom Sr. stood in the driving rain with the scallop muscle balancing on the point of his pocket knife. "Go ahead and try it."

JOHN MENDONCA
Nantucket's Oldest Scalloper

All John Mendonca ever wanted out of life was to be a scalloper. Now eighty-four, he remembers going scalloping in 1910 in Nantucket Harbor when the scallops were so thick on the bottom they looked like "the cobblestones on Main Street."

He craved a life as a scalloper but his mother had other plans for him.

His mother hated the water. She would get seasick on land just watching a boat at sea. "My dad was a whaling captain. He married my mom and then, boom, he was gone for four years. When he returned she said, 'Nothing doing, either give up whaling or give up me.' He became a farmer.

"She weighed only ninety pounds but she was no weakling. I told her I wanted to be a fisherman and my mother, who was a half-pint, said, 'You're going to school and you're going to college if I have to take you this way.' Then she took my ear and twisted it till it bent over. 'Don't talk to me about being a fisherman again. Do you understand?' And I never talked to her about it again."

And so instead of dredging the harbor he trudged through Harvard Yard to his masters in guidance counseling.

But now, having survived fifty-four years of guidance counseling in New York City, he's back out there, Nantucket's oldest scalloper, looking and talking like the Wizard of Oz. Up before six, rain or shine, he's answering his partner Jim Crocker's get-ready call on the first vibration of the first ring.

And he no longer has any family restraints. Now that he has fulfilled his mother's plans for him, his wife, Loretta, is proud to have a scalloper for a husband. "I think my husband would rather have scalloped than gone to Harvard," she said.

With a full head of white hair, a healthy tan, and a mean backhand developed on his private tennis court, Mendonca hardly looks like a man born in another century (1898).

Yet he recalls selling lobsters from a horse-drawn wagon for twenty-five cents each, regardless of size, to the summer people in Sconset. "Islanders didn't buy lobsters. If they wanted a lobster they'd

tell Jesse (his fishing mentor). He'd pick up a five-pound lobster and throw it to them. No money."

Mendonca sliced himself a piece of cranberry nut bread and looked out the back of his Pocomo house, past the green tennis court and toward the water. "I built this house for $298 in 1928." The land the house sits on cost $50. Years later when a neighbor died, he bought more waterfront land for $1,000. Recently he was offered $280,000 for his property and refused it.

Mendonca reacted sharply toward the construction boom on the island. "Nantucketers blame outsiders for this buildup but it's our own fault. A lot of this is greed, just plain greed."

"In 1909 we used to get one-fifty a gallon for scallops. Once in a while we'd get three dollars a gallon. Now they get forty-five a gallon. It's crazy."

Now when he has a particularly good day, Mendonca opens his scallops and brings a bunch over to Our Island Home. But it's not as easy as in the good old days. "You could go out and make a short tow and you'd pull up the dredges and find practically all scallops. There wasn't

any junk [seaweed] in the thing. We got so many once that the skiff we had, which was a big working skiff, sank. The unenforced limit then was twenty bushels to a man, forty to a boat, compared to six bushels per man, twelve per boat presently enforced."

Mendonca returned to scalloping in 1979 at the age of eighty-one. "During the warm sunny days at the beginning of the season in November [scallop season is November to April], I heard some of those younger guys whispering 'wait till it gets cold' in my direction. But I went every day it was goable. I never got tired of it. I'm going to do it next year, too."

From the *Inquirer Mirror* 1901

Down t'the Room of leisure day —
The Cap'ns tell their stories —
Tales of their by-gone whaling days.
Full of salt sea glories —
Tales of the days that have passed away
That are never more returning,
When hearts of the boys of this old town
With love for the sea were burning.
Wrinkled and gray, though these Cap'ns bold.
A light in their eyes still gleaming —
They spin the yarns of their voyages old, —
Truth stronger than fiction seeming.
Stranded at last in the old home port,
Their long voyages over,
May they end their days in rest and peace —
Each grand old ocean rover.

Nancy Grant Adams

DEER/FERRY

If Nantucket Sound ever were to divide like the Red Sea, early December would be the time. From the appearance of the two groups heading for the Sunday-afternoon Steamship, it looks like trouble in paradise.

First comes the Beacon Hill–Sutton Place crowd, carrying Nantucket lightship baskets and buttoning up Lord and Taylor fur coats. They have braved the chilly December air the previous night for Christmas Stroll, and so they quickly scurry into the warmth of the Steamship Authority terminal.

Then comes the deer-hunting–four-wheel-drive crowd from Cape Cod. In their eyes, status means a large doe or buck tied to the roof of their Jeeps. The day before, they had clambered through the thick oak brush of the moors on the last official day of deer-hunting season. Now they stand in small groups outside their Jeeps, oblivious to the cold, trading hunting tales.

The Beacon Hill–Sutton Place crowd sweeps from the terminal just as the deer hunters begin driving their vehicles aboard the *Uncatena*. The two groups exchange angry stares.

"You know," sighs one hunter, "they waste five or six hundred dollars on those silly handmade baskets. Why, if I had six hundred dollars I'd be down in Islamorada in the sunny Keys, swordfishing with Ted Williams."

A late arrival, dressed in a black- and red-checked peacoat, heads quickly down Broad Street toward the ferry. For luggage, he has a skinny doe, mangled by several shots, draped around his shoulder casually as an August tourist carries a camera.

A woman bursts into his path. "Murderer!" she blurts at him between sobs. "A defenseless baby! How could you?"

"Lady, this island's overpopulated with deer," responds the hunter. "If we don't thin them out, they die of starvation."

"They're so innocent, so beautiful. You're sick," she says bitterly before turning away.

The man looks at her fur coat. "At least I *eat* venison," he mutters.

The woman boards the boat and takes a left. The deer hunter boards and makes a sharp right.

WINTER

The cab driver drove steadily through the silent lanes of Sconset, across the midsection of Nantucket and on into town. During the seven-and-one-half-mile trip, he saw neither another moving car nor a human being. When he reached Washington Street, a Volkswagen occupied the first space at the stop sign. He shook his head sadly and muttered, "Goddam traffic jam."

Only in January on Nantucket could two vehicles at the same stop sign be considered a traffic jam. Although more people are choosing to live year-round here, there are still not enough bodies to disrupt this time of incredible beauty, solitude, and serenity.

The cab driver laughed and said, "I'm seventy-three." Asked why he looked only fifty-five or sixty, he replied, "I live here, that's why. No pressure."

*   *   *

On the beach at Nobadeer, a well-bundled couple walks. A curious gray seal keeps pace, diving under the icy Atlantic

47

and surfacing to look at them again.

In Shimmo, a hawk circles effortlessly against a steel blue sky. In 26-degree chill, the hawk can still forage for food. But not so the scalloper. The dredging for the rest of the scallop harvest must wait by law for the temperature to climb above 28 degrees, or the seed scallops will freeze on the culling board before being thrown back.

It seems sometimes that there are absolutely no sounds. And a tip of the head at night can send you into the outer limits of space, tumbling through constellations never mentioned in astronomy class. From Dionis, the lights of Hyannis shine as if to signal another dimension.

At the Pacific Club, however, it is a dimension of neither sight nor sound, but of time. Old times.

Ralph Dunham sat in a captain's chair with his feet propped up on an old stove. "This guy wakes up the preacher in the middle of the night," Dunham began, "and says, 'Reverend, this is an emergency! I'm going off-island and I have to get married immediately.' The Reverend douses his face with cold water and performs the ceremony. 'Just give me what you think its worth, he tells the newly-wed groom. So the guy digs into his pocket and hands the Reverend a dollar bill. The Reverend takes a good look at the bride, then hands the guy back fifty cents." The room filled with a laughter loud enough to be heard outside, warm enough to cut the December chill.

Snow cannot be counted on every winter. But when it does fall, it usually melts before turning ugly. When it lands on Main Street, the evergreens lining the cobblestone road since early December wear an accent of white.

The trees are purchased annually by the town and put up by the department of public works, which also strings the lights. The decorations are created by island residents and hang on the trees months after the lights are down.

The first lighting comes during the Christmas Stroll, a shopper's delight accompanied by the summer crowd's only off-season return. The shops provide the eggnog, hot buttered rum, and good cheer on the house.

A December storm, recently, stranded two thousand of these Christmas visitors in town, and seventeen whales on the beaches.

*   *   *

On New Years Eve Dick Swain threw another log into the wood stove, adjusted the color on his television set and sank into his favorite chair. The live coverage of Times Square brought a scowl to his face. He had celebrated New Years Eve in Times Square once, thirty years ago, he recalled.

"It's thousands of people jammed together pretending they're having a good time. They're not," he said.

"I got goosed, picked up by the crowd and carried away." He fingered the armchair and poured a glass of straight gin. "I'm staying right here tonight."

Nantucket has no traffic lights and if YOU DESERVE A BREAK TODAY, you can't HAVE IT YOUR WAY. No Dunkin' Donuts either. And why should it be missed? Good coffee and all the gossip you can swallow are served at either Main Street pharmacy any morning.

Gossip is one of the few forms of entertainment. The Dreamland Theater closes its doors soon after Labor Day. And the Gaslight Theater is open only Thursday through Sunday. On many nights, you see not only a film there, but also your own breath. Get the hot popcorn without butter so that your fingers stay warm.

For the high school kids, this is a time when they begin to feel, as one graduate of Nantucket High said, "like there's a world out there and we're missing it." The only diversion for some is to get a couple of six-packs and drive around.

One group of high-spirited graduates allowed me to ride with them in their Jeep one night. The combination of driving, drinking, and playing "Born to Run" at threshold-of-pain volume brought on the police cruiser lights.

Meekly, I asked if we were going to ditch the open beer before pulling over for the cops. "Don't waste your beer," the driver said as he accelerated. The Jeep whipped right off the Polpis Road and headed into the moors. Once in the sand, the cops never had a chance against our four-wheel drive.

We drove rapidly up a hill leading to a summer house and an eighty-foot drop to the ocean. When the headlights slid off the edge of the cliff into darkness, the driver hit the brakes. The Jeep stopped a mere tire revolution from the edge. The driver giggled.

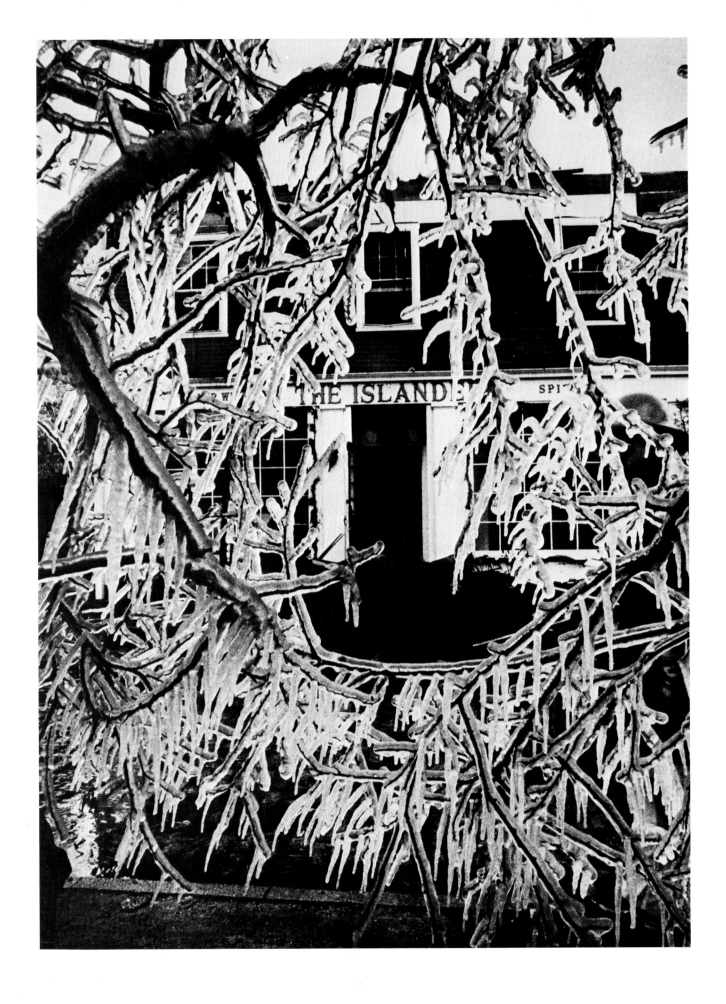

74

What a Tourist Can Do in Nantucket in the Dead of Winter

1. Search for that secret entrance to the tunnel to Hyannis.
2. Buy a swimsuit while it is still on sale.
3. Catch a sunset from the beach at Madaket.
4. Catch pneumonia from the beach at Madaket.
5. Count the cobblestones on Main Street.
6. Go to the front of the Dreamland Theater box office window with the memory of waiting last summer in a four-block line to see *Mary Poppins*. RE-JOICE! Today you are right in front. Unfortunately the Dreamland is closed for the winter.
7. Listen to traffic reports from both New York City and Boston on your car radio. Then reenact the bottleneck on the Harlem River Drive and at the Sumner Tunnel using your car and several hundred empty scallop shells.
8. Denounce the ugly summer crowds: The rich elite buying up the island and destroying its serenity and quaintness. The day-trippers jamming Main Street and Jetties Beach. Long lines. Higher prices. Mopeds and no vacancies. Sticky ice cream splattered on cobblestones. Calvin Kleins swishing down the sidewalks. Alligator shirts pouring off the Steamship like a tidal wave of many colors. Tourists grabbing Nantucket baskets, shirts, pens, ashtrays, and other junk made in Korea. Yachtsmen in ascots, bounding to shore only to dump their trash. Who needs it?
9. Make reservations now for two weeks in July.

BROWNIE

Everybody in Nantucket knows Brownie. He's got the most-photographed face on the island. His picture has appeared in *The Boston Globe*, *The New York Times*, *The Washington Post*, on several television stations, and on a Pierre Cardin fashion catalog. Tourists think he's an old whaling captain. Locals know that he was a scalloper and then a bricklayer before his arthritic knees forced early retirement in 1965.

Now he's up at 4:30 A.M. and down at the wharf every day, weather permitting. He drinks eighteen to twenty nips of straight vodka daily, liver permitting.

Brownie's legs were bothering him so badly once that, reluctantly, he went to the doctor. After the examination the doctor said, "Mr. Browne, I'm afraid you have water on the knee. . . ."

"But that's impossible," Brownie replied. "I haven't had a glass of water in forty years. I must have vodka on the knee!"

Around noon he hobbles bowlegged with his cane up to Main Street, where he occupies a park bench near the Hub. On real nasty winter days he stays home and watches the soap operas. "I like 'em 'cause you can miss a whole summer's worth and catch up on the plot in three days."

Edouard Stackpole, curator of the Peter Foulger Museum, refers to him as a "waterfront philosopher." The Nantucket police occasionally have to put the waterfront philosopher in protective custody when the HyLine boats arrive in the summer.

Folks who know Brownie don't say anything about him that he doesn't say about himself. "Brownie," says Brownie, "raises hell."

Brownie didn't always look photogenic. "I was full of pimples until I was twenty-five. And do you know how I got rid of them — molasses and sulfur. I took that for three days and they cleared right up. But you fart. That's the sulfur, you know."

Born on Nantucket, the only time he's left the island in the past couple of years was for a brief trip to Hyannis. Why Hyannis? "To drink," Brownie replied.

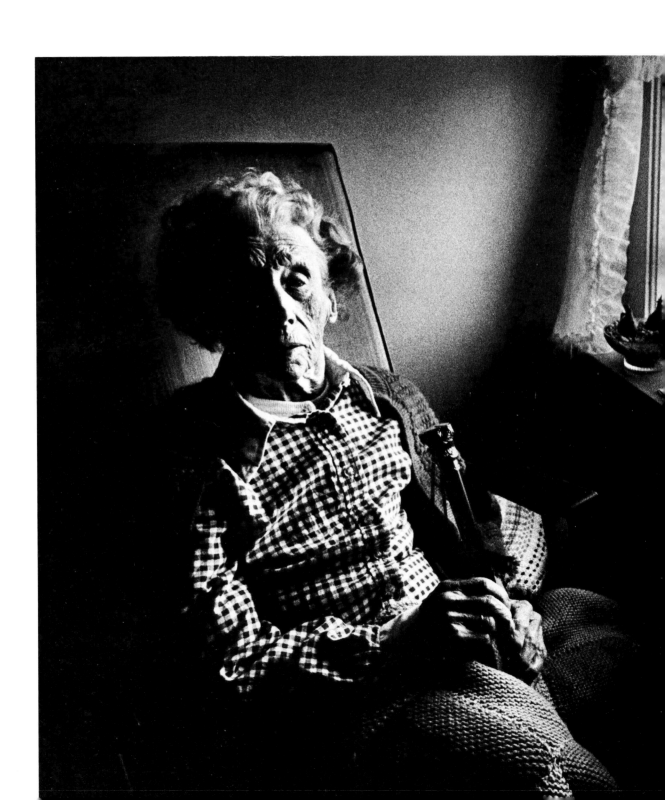

MARY SHERMAN

Mary Sherman twirled the *Boston Post* cane between her fingers and gazed through the lace curtains in her room of Our Island Home.

The cane designated her as Nantucket's oldest resident in a hand-me-down tradition started by the old *Boston Post.* Yet some Islanders felt she didn't deserve it.

One elderly resident of the rest home stood in her bathrobe and shook her head. "She's not an Islander. She doesn't know anything about the island and she doesn't deserve the cane." Another Islander commented that the holder of the cane "usually has one foot in the grave, another on a banana peel."

Yet Mary Howland Sherman was a descendant of Thomas Mayhew, who at one time owned Nantucket.

The deed for the island was sold to him by Lord Sterling in 1641. It called for "free Liberty, and full Power to them [Mayhew and Son] their Heyres, and Assignes forever." But by 1659, Mayhew, obviously with little foresight for the future value of the future resort, sold ninety-five percent of the island for thirty pounds and two beaver hats.

89

"Mayhew never was a resident of Nantucket and no detailed biography seems needed," reads Starbuck's *History of Nantucket.*

Mary Sherman moved to Nantucket in 1948. She was born in East Avon, New York, near Rochester, on September 6, 1883. Mary could sing before she could talk. "I inherited a voice of quality — a beautiful voice, sweet and appealing," she recalled. She used to have her church groups in tears during her solos. She was also interested in politics from the time she heard presidential candidate William Jennings Bryan deliver a speech from the back of an Erie Railroad car in Avon, New York, in 1896. A drawing of hers was exhibited in the Chicago World's Fair of 1893. She rushed through high school and at the age of eighteen was given a special permit to teach elementary school. Except for a cross-country trip she took in 1925, financed by selling shoes out of a Model T Ford, she spent most of her years teaching in country schools until she retired to Nantucket.

She first traveled to Nantucket in 1948 or '46 — she was not sure which — "because it is awfully cute," and to take care of some of the island's elderly. She en-

tered Our Island Home in July, 1974. Five years later, she received the cane honoring her as the island's oldest resident.

"Yes, I'm proud of it," she said, as she ran her fingers over the cane. "It's ebony with a gold head. Pretty, isn't it?"

She paused and turned again to the world beyond her window. In the distance was the harbor, Brant Point lighthouse and the jetties through which steamships, every day, would round the point and come fully into her view.

On this day, there was a distraction in the foreground as workmen in hardhats were busy constructing a building. For Mary and the other residents of Our Island Home, clanging construction was more than a noise irritation; it was a further sign that time was passing them by, and taking the old Nantucket with it. But this construction, right outside their windows, was different. It was a welcome distraction, for the workmen were building a new Our Island Home. "I hope to be carried over the threshold as the first patient in the new home," she said.

She enjoyed Nantucket through all its seasons. "I'm not one of those kinds that gets lonely in the winter. In winter, we read. I'm not a card player, just a little. I don't take to bingo . . ." Mary's voice broke off. She smiled, then continued.

"I'm usually sharp, but not today. Come back again and we'll try to give a more sensitive performance." With that she started singing, "And when I get too old to dream, your love will live in my heart."

There were many things Mary did not reveal about herself that day, most notably that, in her 82nd year, she began writing "Our Story." The 12,000-word manuscript is a remarkable jumble of detailed reminiscences from her own mental scrapbook.

"I always had money from the earliest, to give or to loan, and still have," she wrote in Chapter Eight. "I never thought to invest it for the future but expended it where it was needed. Its investment was in goodwill and that is wholly as satisfying as having an expanded bank account, when it comes to the end of life."

Months after my visit with her, I looked for her when I boarded a frosted school bus, the only vehicle allowed on Main Street during the annual Christmas Stroll. Inside the bus, Our Island Home residents were dispensed small plastic jig-

ger glasses—filled not with eggnog, as the revelers on the street held, but with medicine. For some of the bedridden residents, the Christmas tour of Nantucket was their only venture outside the Home all year. Mary Sherman was not among them. "She wanted so badly to be here," said one of her friends.

A few days earlier Mary had been flown off-island for cancer treatments in Walpole, Massachusetts. She died January 11, 1981.

In her obituary of Mary, Merle Orleans of the *Nantucket Inquirer and Mirror* wrote: "It was one of the few regrets of her active life that she had not been born in Nantucket."

The cane was passed to Lydia Rowley who, when it was presented, blurted, "Does this mean I'm going to die?"

CHANNEL 3 NEWS

MORNING LIVE

JANUARY 12

THE MEMBERS OF THE NANTUCKET WILDLIFE ASSOCIATION ARE PEOPLE WHO ARE REALLY

LOOKING FORWARD TO THE BOAT'S DOCKING...

THEY HAVE GRAIN TO FEED DUCKS ON THE BOAT AND THE ASSOCIATION MEMBERS ARE

PLEADING FOR DONATIONS SO MORE GRAIN CAN BE PURCHASED FOR THE STARVING

WATERFOWL...

YESTERDAY,,,VOLUNTEERS FROM """DUCKS UNLIMITED""" VENTURED TO MADAKET TO

CHAIN-SAW HOLES IN THE ICE SO THE DUCKS CAN DIVE FOR FOOD...

BUT THE HOLES ARE QUICKLY FILLED AGAIN BY ICE...

200 POUNDS OF GRAIN FOR EACH POND ARE NEEDED---HUMMOCK POND, LONG POND,,,

MIACOMET AND SLOSECK'S FARM...

DONATIONS MAY BE MADE TO THE WILDLIFE ASSOCIATION,,,CARE OF SUZANNE

SANGUINETTI,,,54 WASHINGTON ST....

DONATIONS ARE TAX-DEDUCTIBLE...

IN THE SPRING,,,THE ASSOCATION WILL PLANT ITS OWN SEEDS WITH THE HELP OF

MONEY DONATED NOW...

WHEN YOU SEND IN YOUR DONATION,,,REMEMBER TO INCLUDE YOUR COMPLETE NAME

AND ADDRESS SO A RECEIPT MAY BE MAILED BACK TO YOU....

Voyage of the Uncatena

And so it came to pass that the arctic northeast winds blew hard against the glacial deposit of Nantucket. The hard core dug in.

By January the island was finally surrounded by three-foot-thick ice and widespread panic had set in; everywhere that is, but on Nantucket.

From the air it looked like the Ice Age had made a comeback. Solid ice as far as the eye could see between Nantucket and the Cape, thirty miles away.

From somewhere in the middle of Nantucket Sound, a radio message from the *MV Uncatena* to the Coast Guard tug *Yankton* was brief and to the point: "We're stuck," said the captain.

That message traveled through the January arctic air mass to the Coast Guard station at Brant Point on Nantucket, where Officer of the Day Mike Petrosino was preparing the coffee. Four and a half scoops per pot plus a couple of shakes of salt to remove acidity. There wasn't much else Petrosino could do but monitor the radio transmissions: Brant Point ice was a solid three feet thick and its forty-four foot cutter would remain prisoner until mid-March.

"I spent a year stationed in Ketchikan, Alaska," he said, bending down to pet the station's canine, appropriately named Dog. "This stuff never happens there. I wore my heavy Coast Guard jacket with the snorkel hood only twice the whole time I was there. I've had it on three weeks straight here," he said.

"But I'd rather be here. In Ketchikan, a plain cheese pizza goes for nine dollars, they have zero bowling alleys, and *Return of the Giant Killer Tomatoes* is playing all the time at the only movie theater."

The scanner crackled again and Petrosino put down his sixth cup of coffee to adjust the squelch.

Uncatena: "We're picking up speed now."

Yankton: "Looking good from my position."

The *Yankton*, a 1,000-horsepower Coast Guard tug, had been dispatched from South Portland, Maine because Nantucket had been frozen in for three days without ferry service.

The 160-foot *Yankton* would go a hundred yards forward and ram the ice while the tailgating *Uncatena* would try to advance half its length before being ground to a halt by pressure ridges of re-frozen ice. Then the *Uncatena* would back up and surge atop the ice, which would crush under its weight.

"It's like putting your automobile up against a cement wall and stepping on the gas," Pilot Robert Anderson commented to one passenger.

Aboard the *Uncatena*, the crew gave eighty-year-old Gladys Russell a pillow and a blanket. Gladys was returning to her home in Nantucket by boat because she was afraid to fly. She used to tell her friends that "flying should be left to the birds." Her family had picked her up in Boston on Saturday and had driven to Woods Hole only to find the boat canceled. They stayed in a hotel.

On Sunday, Gladys and her family boarded the *Uncatena*, which moved within three miles of Nantucket, got stuck, and finally had to return to Woods Hole. That cruise to nowhere took twelve hours. They rechecked into the Holiday Inn.

"I told them [her family] they should have gotten rid of me then," Gladys Russell said. But Monday morning they were among twenty-two passengers, necessary food supplies, and a determined captain.

They left Woods Hole at 10:00 A.M.

They arrived at 1:40 A.M. The usual crossing time of three hours and fifteen minutes had taken fourteen hours and forty minutes. Captain Edward Nemath, with fifteen years as a captain and more than forty on the seas, called the voyage the longest he had ever seen. He praised the crew, the passengers, and the Coast Guard, and made his way below to a small bunk bed. One passenger said the trip was "neat." Another, a deliveryman from Rhode Island, cursed the boredom and the lost time. Still another described how he threw a beer can overboard to chart the *Uncatena*'s forward progress.

But happiest of all was Gladys Russell. For her and her family it was a sixty-hour journey. Had they headed west out of Boston they could have driven to the sunny beaches of San Jose, California.

But California isn't home. Nantucket is. And who says you can't teach an old dog new tricks? Gladys Russell now thinks she's ready to fly.

*　　*　　*

With the ferry service disrupted by the ice, Nantucket began surfacing in the national news. The whole world was

watching but Nantucketers were at first yawning and then laughing. Did the national news media expect pictures of frozen, tattered natives carrying their firstborn across the ice to Hyannis, followed by a flock of lean, starving sheep?

In a truly biblical sense, the island was receiving manna from heaven, or, more specifically, milk and eggs flown in from Hyannis by local food stores.

Yet, all over the island residents began receiving phone calls about an evacuation from off-island — the result of an erroneous news report. The farthest phone call came from Guam, where a worried Sheila Johnson called her mother, 16,000 miles away on Nantucket.

"She had heard that Nantucket was being evacuated and wanted to know if we needed money or anything," said Mrs. Sina Gomes, an elementary school crossing guard. "They thought we were underwater or something. I had so many offers for care packages I should have kept my big mouth shut. I would have really cleaned up."

Channel Three News Director Ellen Powers traced the rumors to a United Press International story out of Boston quoting a Coast Guard official as saying that if fuel barges could not get through the ice surrounding Nantucket within a few days, one consideration would be to evacuate residents.

By the time that story went out over the air on WCBS News Radio Network in New York, Desk Assistant Tony Gatto said the story read, "Officials fear the almost five thousand inhabitants will have to be evacuated if the fuel barges cannot get through by today."

But, in fact, the 3,000 horsepower Mobil oil barge had little trouble delivering 425,000 gallons of heating oil that day. On Saturday 5,500 pounds of food had been airlifted in. Life proceeded as usual on the tiny frozen island.

Nantucket Fire Chief Bruce Watts received a call from NBC and CBS in New York at 6:30 A.M. "They wanted to know the evacuation plans. I said, 'What evacuation? We don't know nothing about an evacuation and we don't have any problems. It's the people on the mainland who have the problems.'"

Nantucket Police Chief Paul Hunter, who has a penchant for fast food, told Channel Three that if residents were

evacuated he hoped it would be to Wendy's in Hyannis so that everyone could eat double cheeseburgers for two weeks.

Phone calls were reported from at least twenty-two states, Guam, Saudi Arabia, Spain, and England. From Ketchikan, Alaska, a caller reported that it was a balmy fifty-three degrees above zero.

Gary Holmes, then a *Nantucket Inquirer Mirror* reporter, said when he awoke and first heard about the "evacuation," he got the sick feeling in his stomach that comes when a reporter misses a really big story. Later, he was at Nantucket Memorial Airport when the first perishables arrived. The television networks were too.

"One newsperson was reportedly upset that there weren't more Islanders at the airport looking for handouts like some starving orphans. 'These people are treating this like a big joke . . . look at that. They need that food.' Of course his argument would have been taken more seriously if he hadn't been pointing to a carton of donuts and éclairs," Holmes reported.

From the mainland, *The Cape Cod Times* said the incident provided "Much-needed laughter for Nantucket residents who have little enough to laugh about this winter."

"No wonder Nantucketers look down on the rest of us," the editorial concluded.

SPRING

Spring has a sound in Nantucket as the silent melting of the winter ice is replaced by the sharp echo of hammers hitting nails all across the island.

The building boom is on, but not without some controversial restraints. During a recent town meeting in the high school gymnasium, residents voted to restrict the number of residences that can be built each year.

What's more, residents and builders face the problem experienced recently by a builder who wanted approval to put a picture window in the house he was constructing. Like other residents and builders, he had to line up at the Town Building, grab a number, bakery style, and wait to do battle with the Nantucket Historic District Commission.

The commissioners, elected but unpaid, believe their mission is to uphold Nantucket's rich past without compromising its future. But some Islanders complain that the commission members rule arbitrarily — nit-picking on some proposals, giving preferential treatment to others, and fighting among themselves.

The builder, aware of the board's reputation, chose a strategy of deference. "I'm totally supportive of your concepts," he told them politely. As they looked over his plans and offered suggestions, he occasionally remarked, "That's a valid point. Thank you."

Then the members rejected the picture window. "We're here," said one, "to prevent a glaring expanse of glass." The builder patiently explained that a neighbor had no less than five glass windows and doors. The reply: "Two wrongs don't make a right." The builder smiled, thanked the members, rolled up his plan, and left.

Outside, he relaxed his Emily Post etiquette. "Those bastards," he said. "Once they made me change my plans nine times and still they wouldn't approve them. The tenth time I went in there with the original plans and they thought they were just fine."

Back inside the conference room, the members told a Wannacomet Water Company representative that a black water tower could not be repainted sky blue. "It has to be gray."

On the heels of that decision, the members decided to consider court action against one homeowner who ignored all warnings and painted his front door pink. A heavy-set girl, the commission members said, complained that she was so surprised by the pink door that she lost control of her bicycle and flipped over the handlebars.

*   *   *

The first warm winds of spring signal the island's rebirth. Restaurants and shops reopen. Stylish ladies with Nantucket lightship baskets, whose sole problem in life seems to be crossing the cobblestones on Main Street, reappear after hibernation from the chill of winter or lengthy Caribbean vacations.

In March, the Woods Hole, Martha's Vineyard and Nantucket Steamship Authority has already sold out auto space for the August first crossing. That's an all-important date — summer rentals change occupants. By mid-April, college students on recess scour the island to line up summer employment.

"Last year I made the mistake of waiting until June to come here," said a student from Oneonta State College in upstate New York, "and I got stuck with a crummy dishwasher job and two misera-

ble roommates. This year I've already landed a job as maître d' and may even have found myself a mistress."

*   *   *

As spring sweeps the island, hundreds of daffodils planted in the fall leap to life along the roads to Sconset, Polpis, Madaket, and Surfside. Storefronts on Main Street sponsor competitions for the best daffodil windows. There's the Daffodil Parade, then the Daffodil Ball. The band at the ball plays "Johnny B. Goode" for the third time, but nobody cares.

In May, truckloads of trash are collected by high school athletes to pay back the community for its support. As the island scrubs for the summer, Nantucket is friendly, anticipating the new faces that hold promise of another season's fortune.

Come Memorial Day, the tourist onslaught begins. Down at the Steamship Authority, out-of-state autos pour off the ferries, spewing fumes and clogging downtown. Five miles away, some Nantucketers hold their final off-season bash: a two-day Demolition Derby at Miacomet Raceway. For them, it's the last gasp at the real Nantucket before too many people spoil too good an island.

BROWNIE, Part 2

"I'm just Brownie. That's all. My sister calls me Willie. My first name is Wilson. Most people call me Brownie, and some call me Whitey. That's 'cause my hair got white when I was eighteen years old. They made a mistake on me.

"Hey, you know what it cost me with the kids yesterday? Two dollars, in quarters. I give 'em all quarters because I like them."

Stevie Ryder grins at Brownie. "I don't know anybody on this island who has as good a time as he does," Stevie says. "Every day. Well, all but Sundays, huh Brownie? You stay at home on Sundays, don't ya?"

"I look at movies on TV and I ride around with my sister. I'm a very religious person," Brownie says solemnly.

"Yeah, right," interjects a friend. "Sacrilegious. Heard you tied one on yesterday, Stevie."

"Tied one on?" Brownie snorts. "He nearly died. You shouldn't have drank yesterday like you did."

"Drank?" says Stevie. "I shouldn't have come down here. But it was my birthday."

"I told you, you never knew how to drink. I told you that yesterday," Brownie reminds him.

"It looks like water," says Stevie.

"Yeah, it looks like water but it acts differently."

They get to talking about yesterday's events — when Stevie wound up in jail.

Brownie laughs, "In my younger days I might visit the cross-bar 'hotel,' but not now."

"I asked for a glass of water while I was in there," Stevie complains, "and they wouldn't give me any."

"Well, they didn't think you were thirsty," says Brownie. "When Brownie's in there they give him coffee."

"You ask for it?" asks Stevie.

"Well, I'm a taxpayer! You're just bashful. Why the hell didn't you ask?" says Brownie.

"The last time I was there they never fished my back pocket. I had a half pint of vodka in there. So I hid it under the bunk. Later one of them came in to look at me and said, 'Brownie, you don't look any better than when you came in here.'"

Brownie becomes interested in the herring gulls on the wharf.

"Come here, you old cuss. Never mind

107

squawking," he tells the bird. "In the summertime, I hit 'em with my cane. They squeal. Get away, you bastards! I ought to wring your necks."

Brownie twists open another nip. When he drinks, all you can see are several air bubbles before it's empty. But his red, white, and blue eyes are still focusing well enough to spot a circling gull.

"Look out, Stevie! You'll get shit on," Brownie warns. Then he gets thoughtful. "Christ, ain't nature wonderful, Stevie?"

A couple of tourists stroll by and spot Brownie. Out comes the Instamatic camera.

"Let me give you something," Brownie says to them. "You got a pen?" He pulls several color postcards of himself out of his pocket. "I'll sign one." He scribbles his name, then hands the woman a stack of postcards.

"That's terrific. What a nice picture," the woman says. "But I don't need all of them!"

Brownie hands one to Stevie.

"I don't want that ugly picture in my house. It should be my picture on it," grumbles Stevie.

The man reaches into his pocket and hands Brownie a dollar.

"You want me to sign another one?" asks Brownie.

The couple smiles and walks away.

"You see," he tells his friends. "I didn't even ask for it."

A very properly dressed woman named Elizabeth sits down next to Brownie. She's a new resident of the island from Connecticut.

"How come you didn't move into that house for sale next door to me?" Brownie says.

"I thought I was going to. But someone else bought the house," says Elizabeth.

"You would have been a good neighbor," says Brownie.

"I know you would have," she tells him. "I would have had you nailing things together and hanging pictures. I would have kept you busy."

"I would have nailed you too," says Brownie. "Don't you worry."

Brownie twists open another nip. "You want one?" he asks her.

"No dear, I don't. I don't drink at noon-time. Oh dear, these Nantucketers are very durable people. They don't have this in suburbia," she says.

"You've got three to go. You're going to space them out, I hope. You should slow down, you know."

"What do you call slow?" he replies. "I can spell that backwards, W-O-S-L. No, W-O-L-S."

"Spell Wauwinet backwards," he's told.

"Oh Jesus, now," says Brownie.

"I've got to go take a nap," says Elizabeth.

"Can I go with you?" asks Brownie.

"No, I'm sorry," she says firmly. "I really am very tired. I had a dinner party last night," she adds.

"You didn't invite me," remarks Brownie.

"It was a very small party, dear," she says.

"Was there much booze?" he asks.

"Yes," says Elizabeth.

"Well, I wouldn't have come, then. I don't drink at night," says Brownie.

"That's when I drink — at night," says Elizabeth.

"But why do you drink in the daytime and not at night like most people?" a friend asks Brownie.

"Well, I'll tell you. Brownie used to drink nights plenty. But now I have mine in the daytime, then I rest at night and I'm all ready to go out the next day," he says.

"Hi there!" Brownie says to some girls walking by.

"Hi Brownie," they say.

"See, they all know me. Why?"

"Because you're an institution on Nantucket," observes Elizabeth dryly.

"No, I'm a constitution," laughs Brownie.

"Well it takes a lot of constitution to be an institution," says Elizabeth.

CAPTAIN GRANT

Captain Peter Grant, eighty-seven, reached for a cold can of Narragansett beer and pulled the tab. The pop jolted his memory.

"It was a clear September night, in 1928 or '29. We had picked up a load of French champagne and Scotch whiskey in Nova Scotia. I was up on watch with the finest set of binoculars money could buy. Jimmy the Frenchman was below, running the course.

"I thought the Coast Guard could never catch us because my ship had converted airplane engines. Three airplane engines that were two-hundred horsepower each. We were capable of going forty knots.

"When we got to Watch Hill, Rhode Island, well, the Coast Guard had the whole goddamn fleet waiting for us. I had one hand on the steering when they put the light on us and told us to stop. I tried to make a smoke screen, combining oil and pyrene — it smokes the hell out of 'em. I told Jimmy to gun it. Jimmy hit the throttle, and they opened up sixteen rounds of machine-gun fire at us. They gave us holy hell. Jimmy yelled up to me, 'Look at all those red fireflies.' You see, every sixth bullet is just a flare so they could see what they were shooting at. I yelled back at Jimmy, 'The hell with the red ones, worry about the other ones.'

"I heard Jimmy yell out in pain and half collapsed forward on the throttle because we slowed down. I was lying flat out on the deck. Christ, I wasn't about to get up and see what happened. Hell no. It was like they had a hose on us.

"When they stopped firing I ran downstairs. Jimmy had on a wool knit hat. When I lifted it up, there was blood gushing and a piece of his scalp dangling. But the bullet had just grazed him. They got him in a hospital real quick and he was okay.

"They weren't such bad guys, though. They let us take a jug or two with us when they threw us in jail. Hell, we had the armed guard so drunk by 4:00 A.M. that we could have escaped ourselves if we weren't so lit.

"They took us to federal court. Christ, when I heard all the charges I thought I'd spend the rest of my life in jail. They had me for conspiracy, smuggling, possession, and disobeying the Coast Guard.

"They let you plead guilty to one count. I did wind up spending ninety days in jail, but it wasn't so bad. I learned the laundry business there."

Before prohibition Peter Grant was a flounder fisherman. But being a descendant of an adventurous family, he knew he was not destined to lead an ordinary life. Tracing the family tree, it's easy to see why.

His great-grandfather's square-rigger was wrecked off Great Point, Nantucket, in 1810 and the elder Grant trudged safely ashore in kilts from his native Scotland.

His grandfather, Captain Charles Grant, was the most successful whaling master in history. His grandmother, Nancy Grant, was an early and determined heroine of the struggle for women's rights.

His father, Captain George Grant, was known as the last of the American whalemen. The story of how he went streaking down Nantucket's Main Street stark naked, after his dory flipped over in 1865, is still talked about today.

"The first thing I remember was the Spanish-American War," said Grant. "The year was 1898 and the battleships at Newport would practice firing their cannons. Christ, the windows in our place would rattle like hell. I was scared, too. As a little kid I used to build sand forts at Surfside so that the Spanish couldn't land there."

The thought of his childhood seemed to relax Grant. Tall and amazingly spry despite his eighty-seven years, Peter Grant still walks the mile from his son's house, where they live on Fair Street, to the Angler's Club, where he trades tales of old Nantucket.

"I used to go down with flounder to Fulton Fish Market in New York in the Twenties. There was no damn money in that. So I got involved with a bunch of gangsters. One of them was in Al Capone's gang. Well, that started me running.

"It used to take three days to get up to St. Pierre, which is seventeen miles off Newfoundland, and four or five to come back. I used to get a thousand dollars for a trip, plus I'd buy a few cases myself and sneak them on. One time I snuck over fifty bottles of Scotch on for myself plus a bunch of champagne. I made out like a bandit on that trip. They'd buy the stuff in Nova Scotia for six dollars a case and sell it to New York millionaires for a hundred. I was making over thirteen thousand a year. Not bad for the Depression.

"I was caught once in Oyster Bay while unloading. No wonder — it was a finger job. Somebody had set us up. We got caught outside Providence, too. We used to keep a bunch of fish on board just in case the Coast Guard boarded us. These fish were really old, though, and they stunk. The Coast Guard smelled a rat. They went below and found the goodies and towed us in.

"The worst was I got caught by the same judge twice. That damn Judge Moskowitz. That's when I decided to go straight. They kept the *Lincoln*, which was a beautiful seventy-footer. So I got another ship and was going to use it for fishing, but it caught fire and burned. I was broke again so I went back to rum-running. I made a couple more trips raising hell in New York. One time we made a run right near the Manhattan Bridge. We unloaded fifty barrels of Scotch right under the cops' noses," he laughs.

"Then I joined the Coast Guard."

Peter Grant adjusted his blue sailing cap with the anchor insignia, tilted his glasses downward on his bulbous nose, and fidgeted in his captain's chair. His memory, incredibly detailed in some instances, became sporadic and ever-changing in others.

"I retired at sixty-five, and the last twenty years I've been just mucking around. There ain't nothing to do here in the winter but play pinochle, and that's slipping fast too. Nantucket's still God's little acre, but they're spoiling it.

"We were happier years ago even though we didn't have beautiful bathrooms and didn't know what TV was. There was something to do every day, like fishing, church dances and suppers. Now you've got to pay a couple of dollars for a lousy highball. It's crazy," he said.

Peter Grant spends his evenings now talking softly into a cassette tape recorder. He glanced over at the pile of completed cassettes and shook his head. The tapes hold his recollections of three generations of an era that can never return.

"Y'know, a boat just don't look good to me any more," he said.

NATHANIEL BENCHLEY

When Nathaniel Benchley moved to Nantucket year-round in 1969, he did it completely, spending his summers in Sconset and his winters seven miles away, in the town of Nantucket. Even when he moved there, he was no newcomer. He had spent his first summer on Nantucket in 1922 when he visited Sconset with his famous humorist father, Robert Benchley.

His writing career spanned forty years, during which he worked for the New York Herald Tribune *and* Newsweek, *produced fifteen novels and children's books, and wrote biographies of his father and Humphrey Bogart. The island was the thinly disguised setting for many of his works, especially his most celebrated novel,* The Off-Islanders, *which became the movie,* The Russians Are Coming, The Russians Are Coming.

In December 1981, eight months after this interview, Benchley died. He was sixty-six years old.

"What do you want me to tell you?" Nathaniel Benchley asked his guest.

"Do you think you're a better writer now that you're living on Nantucket?"

"I find it easier to write here. You just hole in and pull the shades. If you got to looking out the window, you'd never get anything done. If you're going to write, you simply do it. Set aside a period every day and just get at it.

"Of course, Nantucket has a tendency to creep into what I write. It depends on the piece or the book. There was no way to get it into the Bogart book, for instance, and in some of the other novels it just wouldn't be appropriate.

"But in some ways it is harder to get ideas on Nantucket. And in the summer, it's harder to work. In the summer we flatly refuse to go to cocktail parties. If you go to one, you've got to go to them all. It is harder to hole in during the summer. People you haven't seen in a long time come here and you don't want to miss them completely. July and August are really bad."

"Do you think it takes a special breed to live here in the winter?"

"Well, you have to have some resources of your own. The insularity that is bred here is something you have to watch out for. A friend of mine came to live here. All he could do was play golf. He found himself sitting in front of the TV watching basketball and drinking martinis."

"Don't you feel trapped sometimes on this island?"

"We go off-island. We'll take a week off, a few days, or go for months. Sometimes I do books that require research. When I was doing the Bogart book, a lot of people I had to interview were in London. I used that as a good excuse to get away."

"Is there a mystique about being an Islander?"

"There's no mystique about being born and bred here. It's just an accident of your parents' being in the right place."

"Isn't there a story about a guy whose parents were off-island, on vacation, when they had him? Then, when they brought him back, he wasn't considered an Islander?"

"Yes, that's a story I've heard. I don't know if it's true. But I do know that you have to be born here. If you're not born here, that's all there is to it. You're not an Islander."

"Are you treated differently if you're not an Islander?"

"Sometimes. There are a lot of people here now who are in the middle of things, even though they weren't born here. But it is like a club, you know, so they can say 'Us' and 'Them.'"

"Are there still people who have never left the island?"

"No, in the old days some of the old guys never left, but not now. Especially when the draft was on, kids would have to go off-island. Buzzy Coffin was slated to take his father's place as the garbage man in Sconset. But he went into the Air Force and became a radar technician. He never would have gone off the island if it hadn't been for the service. I don't know anyone who doesn't get off now and then."

"The search for Dr. Kilcoyne, who mysteriously disappeared a couple of winters ago, seemed almost out of your book, *Sweet Anarchy.* It was almost prophetic, like you were writing parts of the future of Nantucket, too. The Kilcoyne disappearance was a page-one story if I ever saw one, but during the first week it was buried inside the paper."

"Well, they like to pretend there's no ugly news on Nantucket," said Benchley. "When Jim Crowley was editor of the paper, he found that you were flatly forbidden to say anyone was a suicide. There was a teacher on the island then, though, who had done just that. So Jim wrote the headline, 'Teacher Found Dead. Head in Oven.' Oh, the hate calls he got!

"What sometimes happens is that you

116

think you've invented something outrageous, and then it comes true."

"Did you anticipate the success of *The Russians Are Coming?* Were you happy with the movie?"

"No, I didn't anticipate it. When the book first came out, it was optioned by some movie company and they kept it for about a year and then dropped it. As far as I was concerned, it was just material on the shelf.

"Then word got around that it was a sleeper. I learned long ago not to count on anything. Once you've finished a book and you've done all you can with it, just go on to the next.

"I thought it was a good movie. It wasn't shot here, though. It was made in northern California. The idea obviously came from Nantucket in the book."

"And *Jaws* — did your son Peter expect that?"

"Well, when it was done there was this sudden bidding for it among the movie companies. I remember at one point he had a bid for something like $230,000 and he asked me if he should take it or hold out longer. I told him to grab it and run.

"It's terrible what you have to go through to get a good title. Peter had a hell of a time settling on *Jaws.* He had thousands of choices. No one thought *Jaws* was worth much. He was always saying, apologetically, that you'd have to see it in print. Just saying 'jaws' didn't sound right. Now it has changed the English language — the way people think of the word 'jaws.'"

"When are you happiest on Nantucket?"

"When things calm down in October it's nice. It's quite a contrast here in the fall. The high-society people are still here. They don't mix well with the hunters. That's the beauty of it. You don't have to mix. You can do what you want. There's a whole crowd out in Sconset that I absolutely wouldn't recognize if they walked into the room. They have their life — the golf club and the beach club. And I have my life — The Angler's Club and trying to get another book started."

"What do you do if you sit down at the typewriter and just don't feel like writing?"

"You should write something, because if you don't, you'll find it's harder the next day. But always leave it in the middle of a sentence or an idea. So you get a window to the future."

EDOUARD STACKPOLE, Historian

Edouard Stackpole, seventy-seven, holds the key to Nantucket's past. Stackpole is an Islander, but he quickly dismisses place of birth as a qualification of special significance. "I can't understand why some Nantucketers are so enthralled with their birthplace. It's far overrated. After all, Christ was born in a stable," said Stackpole.

Stackpole loves the island and wants its history understood in the proper historical context. And if that means opening up the Peter Foulger Museum's temperature-controlled research vaults on his day off to answer a nagging question, he cheerfully does it.

Besides being the museum's director, Stackpole has also published twenty books, served as president of the Nantucket Historical Association, and been associate editor of the *Nantucket Inquirer and Mirror.*

"I always tried to be accurate, yet compassionate. A little milk of human kindness never hurt, especially in a small community. The paper would come out on Friday, and by Saturday morning you would meet your major story face to face by chance. So you had to be accurate," he said.

Accuracy is one thing, but settling a friendly dispute between two countries with the stroke of a warm dishcloth is quite another.

During a 1938 dispute between the United States and Great Britain over which nation first laid claim to six islands in the Pacific, Stackpole found original whaleship logs that had been pasted over with scrapbook clippings. His warm dishcloth loosened the flour paste and he removed the scrapbook clippings, enabling him to read the whaleship logs. The dispute was resolved in favor of the United States, Stackpole recalled, when one log dated 1823 revealed that Nantucket Whalemen arrived there that year, before the British.

But his ocean-blue eyes have seen more than just dusty old whaleship captain's logs. As editor of the *Inquirer and Mirror* he covered the tragic story of the loss of the cabin cruiser, *The Constance.*

"It was a September afternoon in 1949. A reverend, his family, and their friends, a total of eleven people, had come over to the island from Falmouth for a picnic," said Stackpole as he ran his hands through his white hair as if to massage his memory.

"They were on their way back to the Cape by 4:30 P.M. when they ran into one of those September squalls. Well, they had a real greenhorn as skipper. He was heading right into driving seas with a big scuttle [a hatch] open. He flooded one engine and then tried to turn broadside and lost the second engine. The raging waters tossed the thirty-eight-foot cabin cruiser. It took on more water. By 5:15 P.M. it had capsized.

"The crew had put on life jackets and tied themselves into a huge ring. The reverend, to keep up everyone's spirits, asked them all to sing.

"The skipper, a guy named Palmer, climbed on the broken roof of the cruiser and eventually washed up at Dionis beach at midnight. He called for help but mistakenly said the crew was out near Tuckernuck Shoal. The night search turned up nothing. Allen Holdgate, who is currently shellfish warden, spotted them several hours later that morning from a plane," Stackpole said.

Holdgate remembers the storm well: "I had a flying service then and was stuck in Falmouth. It was a very localized storm, but a real rip-snorter. I waited around for a while and then decided to fly around it. I went by way of the Vineyard and then approached Nantucket from the south. If I could have gone straight across I would have seen them capsize.

"The next morning I volunteered to patrol. I caught a flash from one of their wristwatches off Dionis. I got my bearings and called the Coast Guard. By that time, there were only four still alive.

"What I saw next was sickening," he recalls. "The Coast Guard approached them from the wrong side. The rope from their jackets got caught in the boat's propeller and dragged two right under. I literally watched them drown. A goddamn shame for that to happen after sixteen hours in the water.

"I could see the boat banging their heads around. It was quite disturbing. I testified at the inquiry that if a problem ever comes up again, I'd call local fishermen. I was sorry I even saw them, because they might have floated ashore," Holdgate said.

The Coast Guard rowed the survivors to Dionis Beach. Edouard Stackpole was there when they came ashore.

"They brought Emily Foster on to the beach first. She looked unconscious," remembers Stackpole. "They placed her face down in the sand and made attempts to revive her. Her fiancé, H. Alfred Allenby, a muscular man, staggered to shore and collapsed.

"When he came to, I asked him if I could get a message to any of his friends. With glazed eyes he looked at me and said, 'Is Emily all right?' I hesitated a second and decided, under the circumstances, to lie. 'Yes,' I replied, but the poor girl had died en route to the hospital.

"Allenby gave me the names of friends in Falmouth. From the friends I got the names of the other crew members who died. I went to Cottage Hospital and interviewed Palmer. He was incoherent.

"Allenby later told me how dark it was when they hit the water. After they formed the ring and the squall had passed they could see lights from the towers on shore. He said he figured they would be reported missing in Falmouth four hours after they left. He described how they sang and how they felt they would all be safely rescued. Then he had

to watch as his sister, mother, father, brother-in-law, and finally his fiancée gave up the ghost. I can still see the grief in his face," Stackpole said.

"Questioning people who have been affected by tragedy is the toughest part of my business," concluded the man who has to preserve the pain as well as the glory of the island.

MADAKET MILLIE, Part 2

The traffic helicopter hovered over the inevitable rush-hour bottleneck on Storrow Drive by Massachusetts General Hospital.

Millie, in a wheelchair, had just finished feeding the ducks along the Charles River. "They're homely," she said. "My ducks may not be better, but they're prettier." She was starting to complain about the cars and the fumes when she heard the chop, chop, chop of the helicopter overhead.

She lifted her shaved, gray head — she had just survived serious brain surgery — and screamed, "Get me the hell out of here, puleeez." Her plea reverberated under the Longfellow Bridge, mixing with the fumes and sounds of Storrow Drive.

Then she cried. She cried out of frustration, having spent most of the summer staring at four walls and a calendar in a hospital room. The helicopter reminded her of the Coast Guard, her dogs, and her home. Each December, the Coast Guard helicopter would land in Millie's yard to drop off her Christmas present.

For Millie, the gift was not the wrapped present — but seeing the chopper in action. As a youngster, Millie loved to hitch up the horse and ride into town. As an oldster, she always wanted to fly in a chopper. The next day she got her chance.

The nurses at MGH nearly went into cardiac arrest when Millie volunteered to take an early morning bath. They helped her dress in her Coast Guard uniform and hugged her goodbye. Millie fed the pigeons in the hospital courtyard one last time, making sure the sickly "wet-look" pigeon got his equal share of corn muffin crumbs.

At the Coast Guard station in Boston's North End, a helicopter waited for her, perched atop a ship like a cherry on an ice-cream sundae.

Millie was placed on a stretcher by eight well-scrubbed Coast Guardsmen and carried up the ship's narrow stairwells. She was seated in a wheelchair and lifted into the chopper, where she was outfitted in a life vest and a headset.

As the engines revved up and the big rotor started to turn, one Coast Guardsman stepped forward and saluted. Millie snapped off a return salute that resembled a karate chop. Then she rolled her eyes toward the heavens and said, "Thank God for the Coast Guard." With that the helicopter trembled, then rose. It was the first of September, Millie's favorite month, and she was heading home.

On warm days, the Coast Guard helicopter usually flies with its big cargo door open — giving the inexperienced flyer a sky-diving sensation. "I'm afraid I'm going to fall," Millie said before they closed the door. "And I have to pee." A brief pit stop was made at Otis Air Force Base on Cape Cod.

On the second leg of the journey, someone pointed out the shores of Chappaquiddick on Martha's Vineyard. "I don't give a shit," Millie said. "I want to see Madaket."

Millie leaned forward as the chopper passed Muskeget, Tuckernuck, and Esther's Island. Esther's used to be part of Madaket until hurricane Esther broke it off in 1961. The shoreline of Madaket had changed rapidly in the last quarter century. The bank of sand that once separated Hither Creek from the volatile Atlantic was gone. So too was the beach grass the local Boy Scouts had planted to halt erosion. Oftentimes, the bridge in

front of Millie's house was under water because of hurricanes. That's the way it was on October 4, 1954 when swells from hurricane Edna washed a ten-foot, ten-inch blue-nosed shark into Hither Creek. Millie remembers that day well.

"I was cutting wood in back of the house when I heard this critter thrashing in the creek. At first I thought it was a sea serpent. All's I could see was a fin sticking up six inches out of the water. But I knew it wasn't something that belonged there. I grabbed a rake and launched a skiff."

Fred Jorgensen got in his boat and Mrs. Jorgensen threw Millie a pitchfork from the partially submerged bridge. The chase was on.

They finally got the shark between Jorgensen's powerboat and Millie's little rubber skiff. "I stuck a pitchfork in him and it goes boom — nothing happens. Their skin is too tough. I don't know if it's tougher than mine 'cause I never stuck a pitchfork in mine. But it's some kind of tough, I know that much.

"He was long and thin . . . very ugly, but he had very handsome, glary eyes," she said. "Every time the big critter came for me and the boat, he'd get a darn good

jab from the pitchfork. It was the most comical setup you'd hope to see. There was no blood or nothin' like that."

The chase took the two boats all through the creek, to both sides of the bridge, and into the reeds. It took the shark an hour and a half to learn something that is common knowledge on the island of Nantucket: You don't mess with Millie.

"We were getting bushed but the big fish finally turned belly-up and surrendered," Millie said. "We towed him ashore and a state trooper put a bullet in him just to make sure he was dead." Millie estimated that the shark weighed three hundred pounds. "We've been kidding everyone about going fishing with their high-class equipment. . . . They tell about the big ones that got away, but we catch the big ones and let the little ones go," she said. "People'd say, 'Oh it was wonderful.' Baloney. It was just a day's job, that's all."

Now the helicopter was hovering six hundred feet above her house. No longer afraid, she ordered the cargo door thrown open. The September air, warm, sweet, and salty, rushed in, replacing the memories of the hospital air conditioning that

Millie loathed.

The pilot, giving the thumbs-up sign from the cockpit, banked the copter at a forty-five-degree angle so that the kingdom of Madaket stretched out before Millie. At first she squinted, then her eyes got bigger as she spotted the West End Command. She leaned forward, extended her seat belt to its limit, and giggled like a sixteen-year-old girl who had just been asked out for the first time.

The sun was sparkling across the waters at Madaket as the helicopter circled. Out at the point, a lone fisherman put down his rod and reel and waved. On the beach, a handful of bikini-clad women made the ultimate sacrifice — they got up from their blankets and waved. An energy-charged youngster raced between blankets, clapping his hands. At Millie's house, neighbor Mary Alice Kahlenbach, who was feeding lunch to the dogs, raced outside, dog food in hand.

Millie absorbed the sunshine, the rolling surf, the salt air, and the serenity of her island paradise. Then, like the Pope appearing in his Vatican window, she waved and bowed to the faithful below.

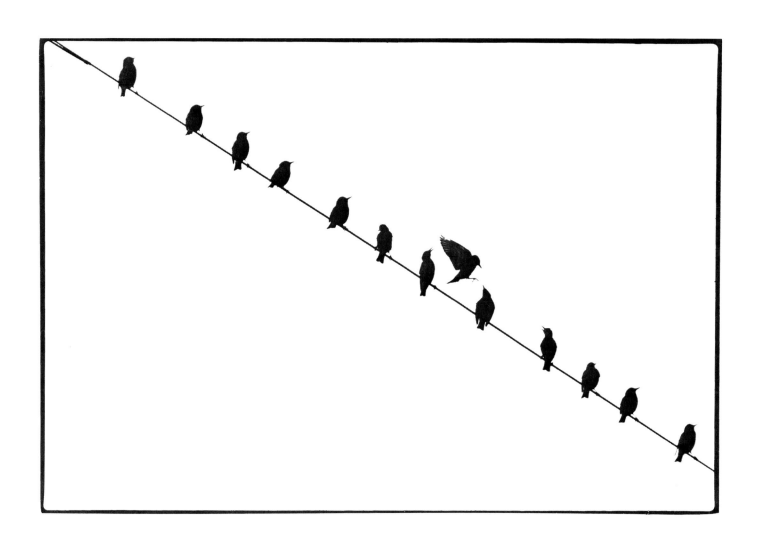